100 Words

Alex Boxall

Copyright 2024 Alex Boxall
Published by J.A.Scott Publications
ISBN: 9798322316145
All Rights Reserved
No part of this book may be reproduced or copied in any way
without the express written permission of the author.

Contents

Introduction

1. Pests
2. Cutting
3. Grief
4. Breakfast in Brazil
5. So Many Friends
6. The Scream
7. My Addiction
8. Silence
9. New Neighbour
10. Swearing
11. Football Teams
12. Tick Tock
13. Church
14. Airport Goodbyes
15. My Empire
16. The Bus Ride
17. Signature
18. Ouija

19. Workout

20. Diet

21. Eyes

22. The Victim

23. Sleeping Beardy

24. Writing

25. Stranger in The Dark

26. The Salesman

27. The Wedding

28. Burglary

29. The Judge

30. First Day

31. The Final Story

About The Author

Other Books by Alex Boxall

Introduction

The barber shop was busy the day I set myself this challenge.

I sat waiting and asked myself if I could write a story with only one hundred words.

A mini-glimpse into someone's life.

Maybe it's my life.

Maybe it's yours.

A tiny tale, or a simple thought.

That's where the story "Cutting" came from.

The rest were written over a period of months.

Sometimes in extended bursts of ADHD induced hyperfocus, and sometimes in snatched seconds between parking up at the school gates and my children getting in the car.

I simply hope each story touches your heart.

1. Pests

I don't invite people to my house anymore.

See, I've got a bit of a problem with pests.

They've over run my house.

And they get into everything.

They get in the pantry, and somehow even the fridge.

I can't tell you how many times I've gone to get myself a biscuit, or some cereal, only to find it's been devoured, only the cardboard box or packet left in place.

I know it's them – they leave crumbs and mess everywhere.

The problem's so bad even pest control can't help.

I can hear one of them in the kitchen now:

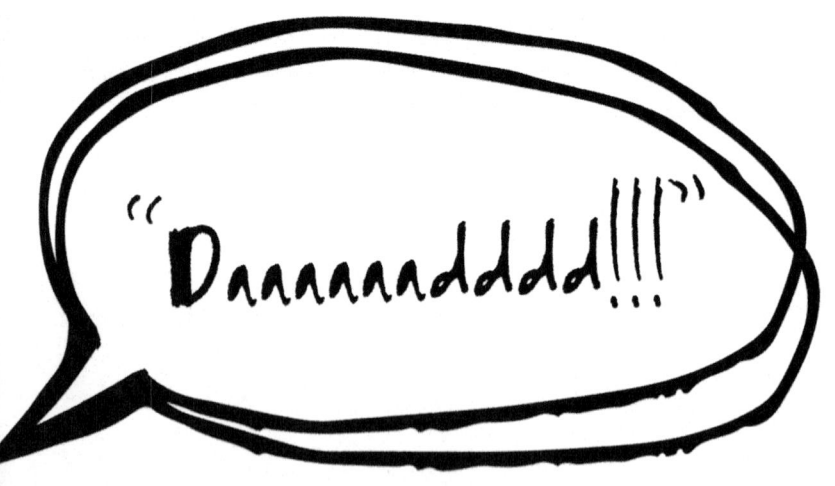

2. Cutting

He lowered his head. He'd had enough of it all.

He'd awoken early, inspired and resolute.

He'd need help.

He couldn't do it himself, but he was used to feeling that way.

He fixed his eyes straight ahead, silent, determined not to flinch.

He watched as the blade was sharpened.

She'd clearly done this before.

He was nervous though.

What if it went wrong?

What if it wasn't a clean cut?

What if this was the wrong decision?

He felt hands on the side of his head, moving him into position:

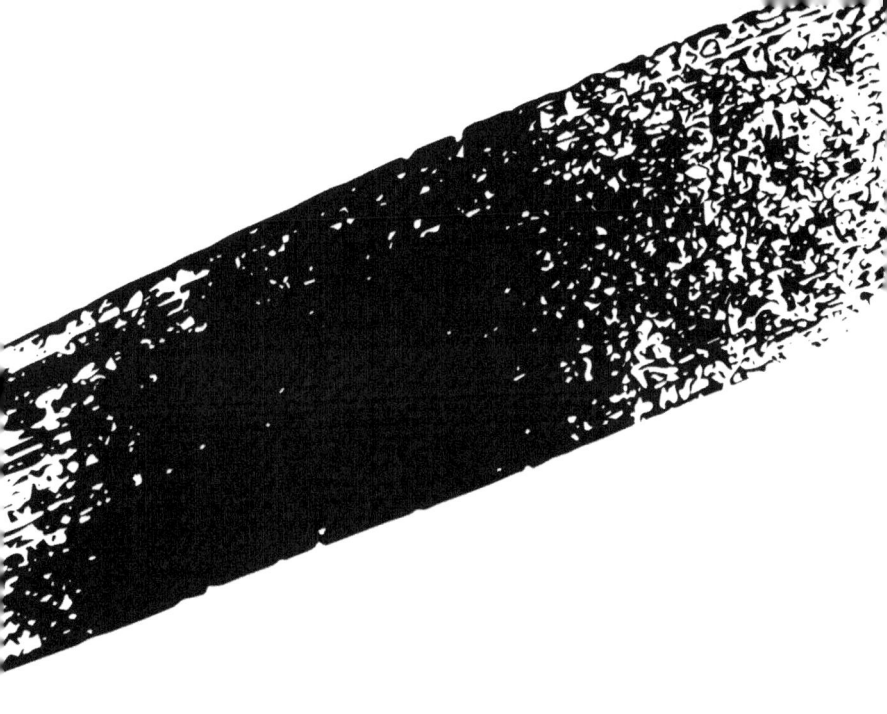

"How would you like your hair cut today, sir?"

5. Grief

The french don't say "I miss you."

They say "Tu me manques."

The literal translation is "You are missing from me."

(They always seem to say things so much better than we do.)

This is what grief feels like.

When you lose a friend,

A lover,

A father, or a mother,

A beloved pet, or even a job.

It's like a piece of the jigsaw puzzle is missing.

Sometimes you find that piece again.

Sometimes it's gone for ever.

Sometimes you forget it's missing.

Sometimes the dark space is all you can see.

The truth?

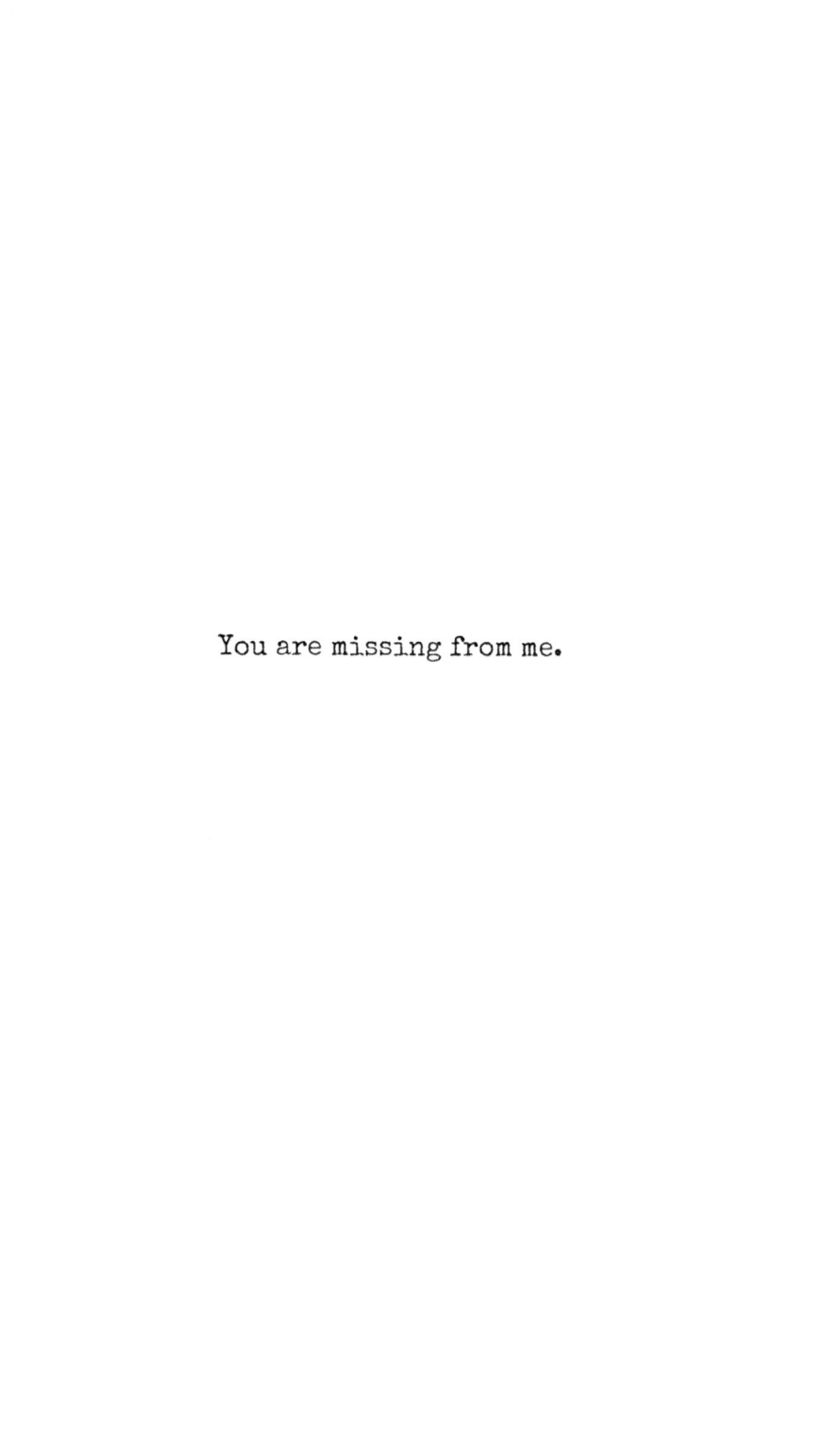

You are missing from me.

4. Breakfast in Brazil

Fresh bread.

Ham.

Cheese.

Oranges.

Tangerines.

Mango.

Papaya.

Apples and Bananas.

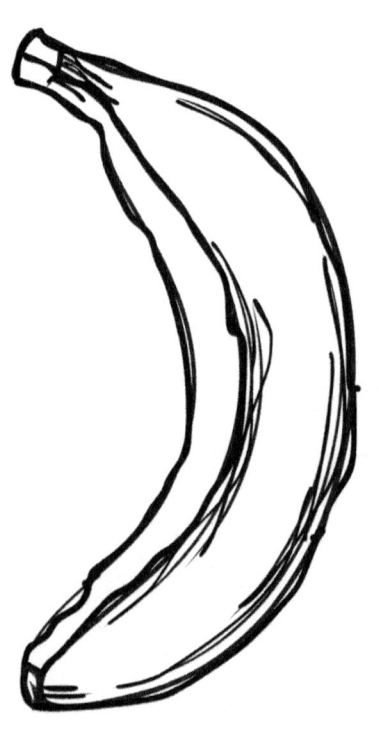

And cake.

There's even cake.

And the clearest honey I've ever seen.

And coffee.

Every juice imaginable.

Fresh melon, cut into cubes, fills a bowl.

Slices of Salami and fresh cream cheese.

The table on the balcony is loaded to the brim.

(Why is there cake?)

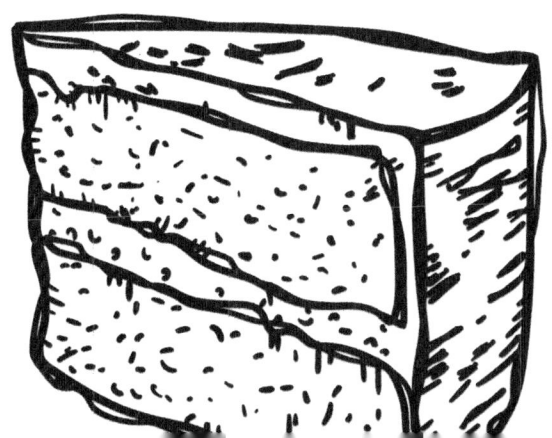

The Brazilian sun, already high in the sky is warming the chairs, shining brightly on everything and everyone.

My ginger skin means this breakfast comes with a sunburn too.

When all I really want are two Weetabix drenched in far too much milk.

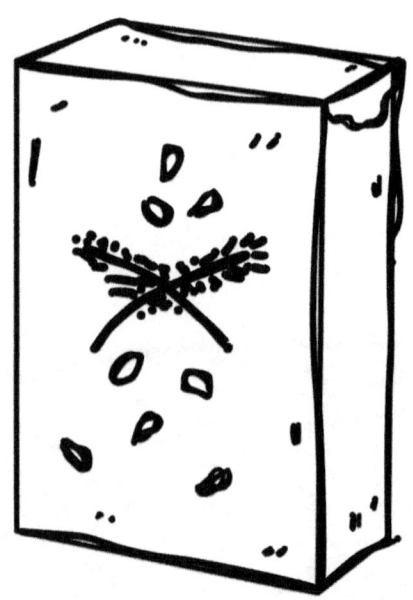

5. So many friends

I have so many friends.

All over the world.

I have friends in Italy.

Friends in Romania.

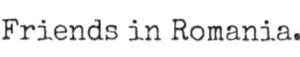

Friends in France.

I've got so many friends in the US I don't think I can count them.

And you wouldn't believe how well I know them all.

I know all their children's names.

I know what they ate for dinner for their anniversaries at the restaurant.

I congratulate them whenever they get a new job.

Or when they become grandparents.

Or their children get married.

And they all know me too.

I have so many friends.

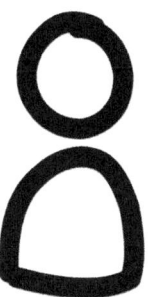

And yet I'm still so alone.

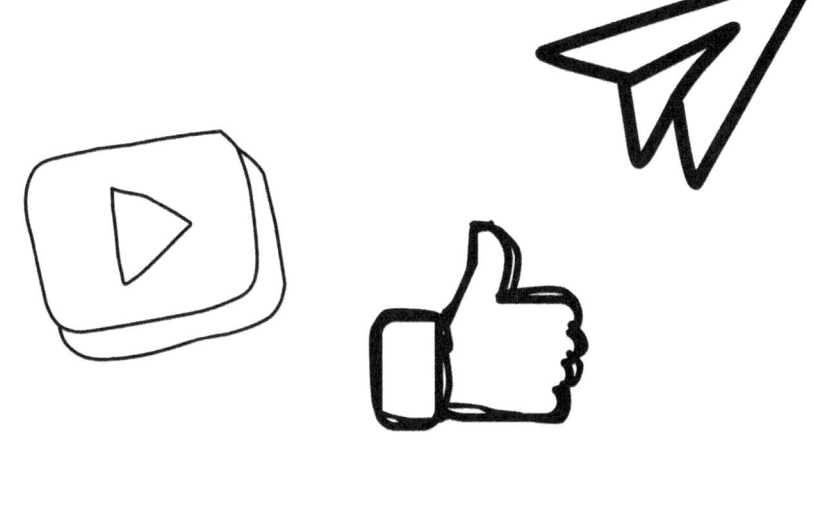

b. The scream

A blood-curdling scream pierces the silence, waking me.

In the darkness I don't want to open my eyes.

Another scream.

That same sound has haunted my dreams for the past three weeks.

It's always unexpected.

I've lived in the same house for years.

I know all the sounds this house makes.

The whumph of the boiler as it ignites,

the gurgling pipes as the heating comes on,

the creaks of the rafters in every strong wind.

Yet another scream.

I feel for my wife in the dark.

She whispers:

"It's your turn to get up.

I fed her last time."

7. My Addiction

I can't wait to get home.

This one should last a while.

Only a couple of blocks to walk and I'll be back.

In my mind I imagine the waves of pleasure that will soon be washing over me.

The children won't be home from school yet.

Maybe I'll allow myself to drift off on the sofa.

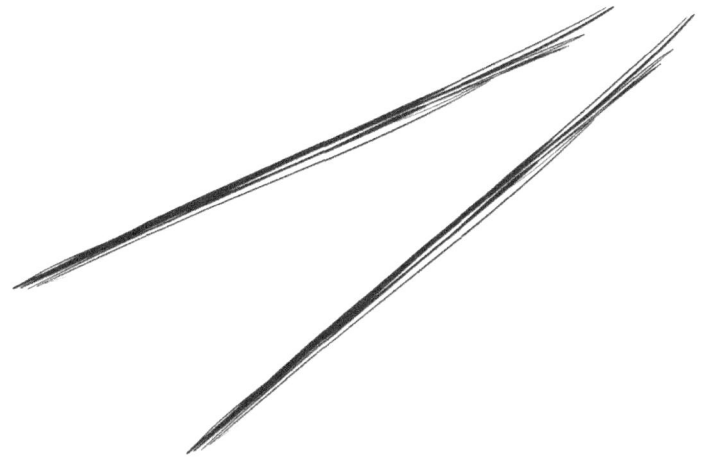

I'm home.

At last.

I make sure everything's clean and get the needle in exactly the right place.

With an easy push it quickly finds its vein.

A crackle, a pop, and

seconds later

my eyes close

8. silence ,

I sink into the silence

The   O

                space

                            between

                                          the

                                                      words

 I listen to the full stops

And dwell on exclamations

Every comma is a verb

I sink into the silence

Into those moments between tracks

Between the crackles and

Between the pops

And every time the needle stops

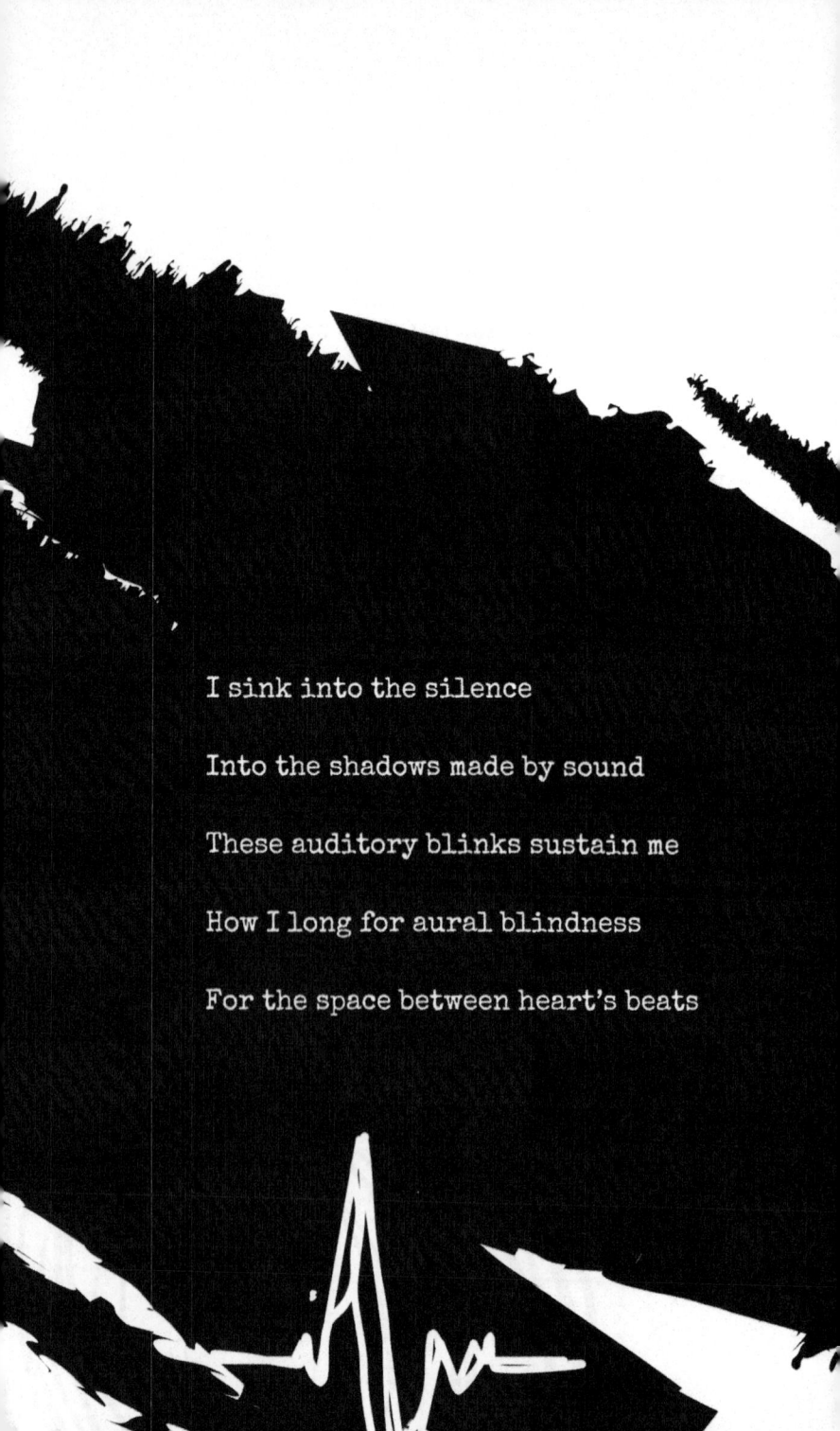

I sink into the silence

Into the shadows made by sound

These auditory blinks sustain me

How I long for aural blindness

For the space between heart's beats

And here,

in this space between the sounds

I find my peace

In the silence

I am still

I am whole

I am

I

,

.

!

9. New Neighbour

She moved in a week ago.

And she's not been round to say hello yet.

I don't think she likes me.

I've noticed she closes the curtains whenever I'm home.

I've waved a couple of times.

She never waves back.

I imagine I won't be getting a Christmas card this year.

I left her a welcome gift on her doorstep but she didn't come to the door when I rang the bell.

She called the police when I tapped on her bedroom window.

And now I'm in a cell.

They seized my binoculars too.

> I don't think she likes me.

10. swearing

Swearing has always been forbidden - religion does that.
However long I can remember,
I've always been told not to swear, not to use those four-letter words
Today, however, I swear a lot, maybe too much.

For too long I was naive and innocent.
Unknown words with unknown meanings stumped me.
Call me a prude, call me an idiot, but I clearly wasn't well read enoug
Knowledge is power they say - knowledge of words even more so.

Obviously I've learned them all now - every single one.
Foreign to my upbringing, they now roll off the tongue, like
Fireworks peppering my conversations.

11. Football Teams

It was always the same.

Playground football.

It should have been so simple.

So fun.

Two captains.

Four players per team.

A quick game of rock, paper, scissors.

Then picking the players.

"You."

"You."

"You."

"You."

"I'll have Bruno."

"John."

Just two of us left now.

Maria's tiny.

And two years younger.

I'm not quite sure how she ended up in the line up with us.

She doesn't even like football.

She looks at me and smiles.

"I'll take... Maria."

"Shit. That's not fair."

He points.

"You might as well have 'Whitey' too. I don't want him."

Playground football hurts.

12. Tick Tock

7:35

A lot to do today.

Tick Tock

                        Swipe

                        Swipe

                        Swipe
                        Swipe
                        Swipe
                        Swipe

                         Like

                        Swipe

                        Swipe

Swipe
Swipe
Swipe

Swipe
Swipe

Like

Send

Swipe
Swipe
Swipe
Swipe
Swipe

Swipe
Swipe

Swipe
Swipe

Swipe
Swipe

Like

Send
Swipe
Swipe

Swipe
Swipe
Swipe
Swipe

Like

Swipe
Swipe

Swipe
Swipe
Swipe
Swipe
Swipe
Swipe

Swipe

Swipe

Swipe

Like
Follow
Swipe

Swipe
Swipe

Swipe
Swipe
Swipe
Swipe

Swipe
Swipe
Swipe

Like
Swipe

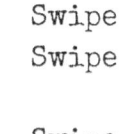

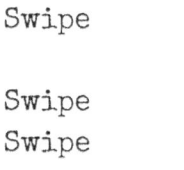

Swipe
Swipe

Swipe

Like
Swipe
Swipe

Like
Swipe

Like

Swipe

Like
Swipe

Like

Swipe

Buy
Swipe
Like

Swipe
Like
Swipe
Buy

Swipe

10:27

Not much time today.

Tik Tok

13. Church

It was Peter who first stepped out onto the waves.

Eyes fixed intently on his teacher, his tentative steps held fast and he stood strong upon the surface of the deep.

His companions followed suit and soon they too all stood upon the water.

As crowds started to gather on the shore of the Great Lake, excitement overtook them.

"Look at me," cried one of them, "it's a miracle!"

"And look at me!" said another.

Soon all twelve were shouting and waving, vying for the attention of the masses.

No one noticed as their teacher slowly sank into the sea.

14. Airport goodbyes

He never thought this day would come.

His parents had always seemed so stayed.

So permanent.

So present.

And yet here they were, suitcases in hand, passports in pockets, standing at the gates, bound for far off foreign lands.

His father's voice falters:

"You will come see us, won't you?"

He knows he won't.

He's always been too afraid to fly.

In fact, the airport was the furthest he had ever been outside his home town.

Driving them here had put him far outside his comfort zone.

A sacrifice he had felt compelled to make.

He never saw them again.

15. My Empire

All of this is mine.

This bedroom,

This bed,

This bathroom.

It's all mine.

This sofa,

This living room,

This kitchen,

All mine.

I earned this.

I deserve this.

Every inch of this space.

Every inch of carpet.

Every corner

Of every room.

And you know what I love most

About all of this beautiful house?

It was a gift.

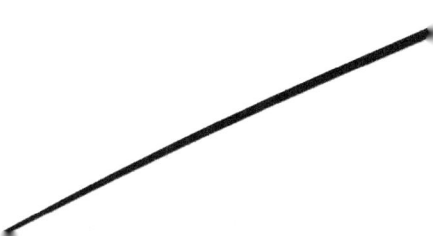

My housemates clubbed together

And bought me this house.

The only stipulation is that they get to live here too.

But I don't mind.

They keep it clean

And share their food.

They're here now.

Best I say hello:

Miaow!

16. The bus Ride

The old man gets on my bus every morning.

Newspaper under his arm as he waves his wife goodbye.

They must have been married for ever.

He hands over the exact change as he smiles at me and says "Return to town, please."

He always thanks me.

He has deep laughter lines around his bright blue eyes and his wispy white hair pokes out from under his flat cap as he shuffles slowly to his seat.

The same seat, every day.

It's raining as I pull up to his stop.

But today he isn't there.

I'll never see him again.

17. signature

He never truly belonged.

He remembered holding his mother's hand, his tiny fingers clasping hers as she cried, begging the stranger to leave him.

His grip failed him.

His four year old body couldn't fight the moustachioed man's muscular arms.

Over time the memory of her face faded as new joys were found.

A red bicycle.

A candle on a cake.

The warm embrace of a new mother.

A new father.

But nothing was ever permanent.

Never forever.

Not until the signature on the piece of paper, seven years in the making.

Only then did he know:

> Finally he belonged.

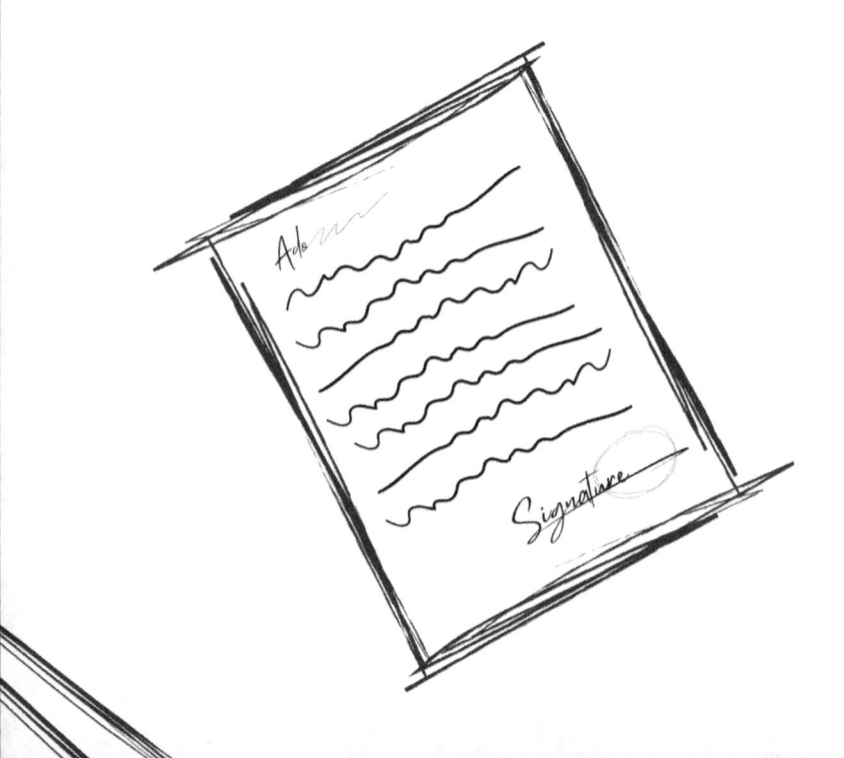

18. Ouija

We met in the abandoned house at the end of our road.

It was early evening and the sun was setting.

Hannah brought the board and the glass.

I brought the candles.

We sat in a circle, the candle flames flickering around us as we each put a finger on the glass.

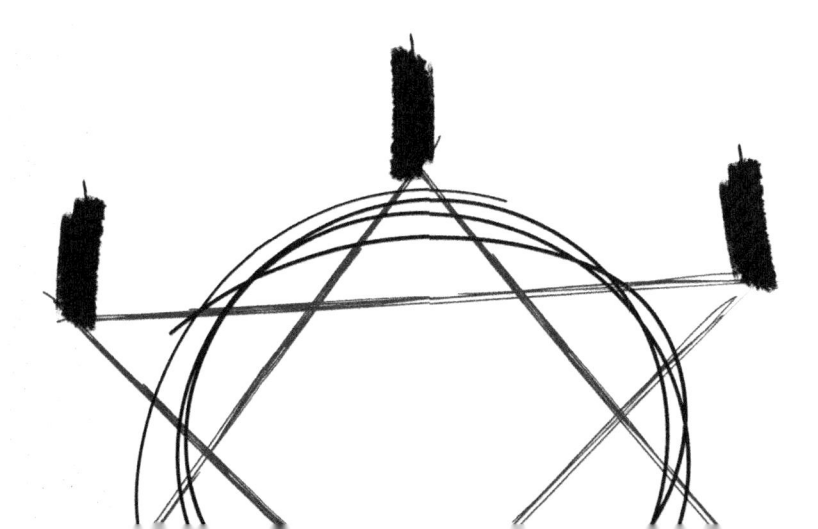

"Speak to us," Giles said, and I felt the glass move.

Slowly at first.

Just a twitch.

Then, with a clear decisiveness, the empty vessel slid slowly to the first letter.

D

Then faster,

i

n

n

E

R

Time

It was my dead mum.

19. Workout

I need more weight.

I've been eating right.

I've been training right.

I've been doing everything and I still can't increase the weight.

I've been stuck here for months.

I know they say there are plateaus, that eventually it'll happen,

but I've been stuck here for so long.

Every time I come to the gym I see people adding weight.

They look so good.

So strong.

It's so impressive.

And here I am.

Still on the same weight.

Day after day.

Week after week.

If it doesn't happen soon,

I think I'll just give up.

Deadlifts are so bloody hard.

20. Diet

I need less weight.

I've been eating right.

I've been training right.

I've been doing everything and I still can't lose the weight.

I've been stuck here for months.

I know they say there are plateaus, that eventually it'll happen,

but I've been stuck here for so long.

Every time I come to the gym I see people losing weight.

They look so good.

So slim.

It's so impressive.

And here I am.

Still at the same weight.

Day after day.

Week after week.

If it doesn't happen soon,

I think I'll just give up.

Dieting is so bloody hard.

21. Eyes

She woke early, tip-toed to the bathroom and put her make up on.

She wanted to look perfect for him.

This had become their routine since they first met just three weeks ago.

She now knew he'd be there every morning.

She knew, if she made it hot and steamy, he would come.

She washed with a smile, cleaning everything, making sure she was ready for him.

She couldn't wait to see that twinkle in his eye.

When she was ready she opened up for him and he entered.

"A large black americano please,"
he said.

She took his order.

22. The Victim

It's not my fault.
They're all out to get me.
The government isn't giving me enough money.
The other driver wasn't looking where he was going.
The teacher doesn't like me.
It's my upbringing.
It's my parent's fault.
My boss has it in for me.
He shouldn't have done that.
It's her fault.
It's their fault.
I'm not to blame.
I wasn't responsible for that.
It was someone else.
It's not fair.
No one listens to me.
Of course they chose her.
It's obviously because I'm not black,
disabled, gay, or a foreigner.
It's not my fault.
I'll never change.

23. Sleeping Beardy

To king and queen a prince was born,
the joy of all the land.

Yet no invite for the evil witch,
so she cursed the babe to hell.

And as foretold, the proud young boy,
before becoming man,

Cut himself on razor's blade,
and into slumber fell.

For fifteen years the prince lay still,
just as was always feared,

'Til fair princess, by happenstance,
found him sleeping there.

She looked upon his hirsute face,
his scraggly unkempt beard,

Recoiling thus, she exclaimed aloud,
"I can't kiss that much hair!"

So the prince,

safe from assault,

lies dormant to this day.

ZZZZZZ

24. Writing

I sit down at my desk again.

I call it my writing desk.

More often than not it's a "waiting desk."

The place where I sit and stare at a screen, watching the cursor blink incessantly on the blank page.

Sometimes the words tumble out, landing luxuriously on the keys of my well worn keyboard, filling my screen with fantastical stories, fabulous fables, or simply a description that brings imagined worlds to life.

More often than not, I languish in the cacophony of my thoughts, struggling to separate the stories from the noise.

But I'll sit here until I do.

25. Stranger in the Dark

She doesn't know him.

She's only here for one day.

Just visiting for work.

A late evening walk in the park should be perfectly safe.

She knows it isn't really.

She can hear his footsteps getting closer.

Her heart starts racing as his heavy breathing gets louder.

She really hopes he hasn't seen her.

Too late.

It becomes obvious he spotted her.

Their eyes lock and she breaks out into a run.

He's running too.

Something in his eyes tells her he won't be giving up easily.

The gap's closing fast.

Then it's over.

As her knife pierces his heart.

26. The salesman

Knock knock.

"Good morning! Can I interest you…"

Slam.

Knock knock.

"Good morning, madam! Have you ever…"

"I'm not interested."

"But…"

"Sorry, I'm not interested."

Slam.

Knock kno…

NO COLD CALLERS

Knock knock.

Knock knock.

"Good morning, sir!"

"Sorry I was in the bathroom."

"That's ok. Good morning, sir, have you ever considered…"

Slam.

Cold cheese and ham sandwich.

Knock knock.

"Good afternoo–"

Slam.

Knock knock.

"Good afternoon, madam, have you ever thought about –"

"Not today."

Slam.

I don't even know what I'm selling anymore.

Knock knock.

No answer.

She's changed the locks.

Guess I'm sleeping in my car again.

27. The Wedding

"If anyone knows of any reason why these two should not be wed, speak now or forever hold your peace."

Should I say something?

The bride looks around the room, resplendent in her beautiful white wedding dress.

Her bright green eyes catch mine and she smiles.

Can I really let this go through?

Should I object?

I'll ruin everyone's day, but will I be able to live with myself if I don't?

The priest looks at us all, smiling.

He's probably done hundreds of these with no objections.

I let go of my bride's hand and raise mine:

"I object."

28. Burglary

The door opens with barely a sound and I step inside.

It's always the same:

house in darkness, no lights on.

From upstairs only the sound of gentle snoring.

They're all asleep.

My well trained footsteps make no sound as I cross the threshold and enter the house.

I climb the stairs.

Slow and calm, until without warning a loud creak fills the silence and I pause, holding my breath.

No sound.

No movement.

I reach the top and creep into the bedroom.

Taking off my police uniform,

    I crawl under the covers,

        where my wife

            is still sound asleep.

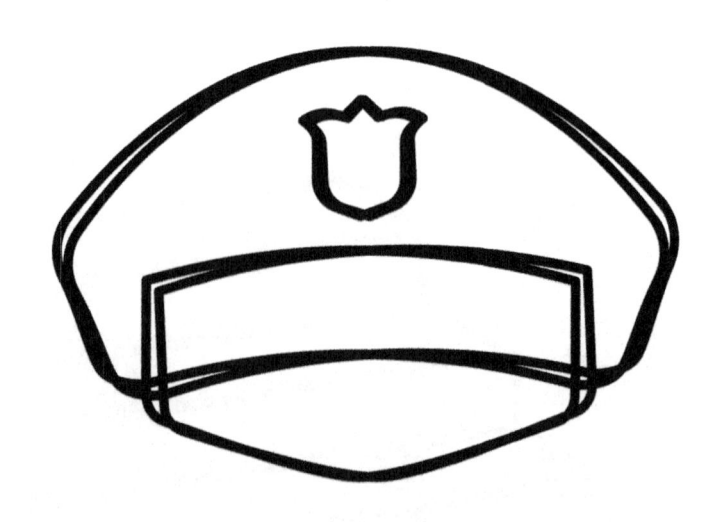

29. The Judge

I hate how he looks at me.

I hate what he's done to all those people.

I can tell he's judging me, just as I'm judging him.

His eyes are full of disdain.

Full of hatred.

I know he knows what I've done.

But I've seen what he's done too.

I know how many families he's torn apart with his callous, careless actions.

How many children will grow up without a parent because of him?

How many people are suffering with PTSD because of him?

It's his turn to speak now.

I show respect and listen:

"Guilty. Take him away."

30. First Day

It all feels so strange.

Walking into an office that looks like every other office I've worked in.

And yet...

I don't recognise anyone.

The inspirational management posters are the same as they always are.

But I don't recognise anyone.

Here desktop computers on individual desks have been replaced by laptops on long benches, but it's otherwise the same as usual.

I try to get their attention.

No one gets up to greet me.

They're all busy.

I just feel awkward.

And I can't remember anyone's name.

So, after thirty-five years, I walk out;

alone,

and unnoticed...

Into the unknown.

31. The Final Story

Sooner or later, it had to happen.

There was no way to avoid it.

No amount of fancy footwork,

wonderful wordplay,

or extraordinary escapism

could render this truth untrue.

Everything must eventually reach this point.

All stories, all tales,

all journeys, all quests –

all doomed to this same fate.

But I have discovered a secret.

There is a way to circumnavigate this most unavoidable finish.

A way to cheat death.

(Or, at least, the death of this book.)

And it's almost too simple.

If you'd like this book to never stop,

do not read the next two words:

The End

About The Author

Alex Boxall wrote this book.

He's written other books too.

Not many, but a few.

They're probably listed on the next pages.

I guess that makes him an author.

He's written songs too.

And on occasion he likes to draw.
Most of the time, however, he spends his days doing marvellously mundane things.

He goes to work, drives a car, struggles with his weight, and scrolls on his phone.

He avoids DIY as much as possible, and clears up cat poo when the cat stands in the litter tray and somehow completely misses the target.

He also has a family.

www.alexboxall.co.uk
x.com/alexboxall
tiktok.com/alexboxallauthor
Instagram.com/alexboxall

Other Books by Alex Boxall

The Last Nephilim

"An excellent read, I struggled to put it down and found myself putting aside other tasks just to read a bit more..."

– Tracy Earle, Author of Darkness Rising

★ ★ ★ ★ ★

Other than the nightmares, and the expensive boarding school, Gabi was just like any other British teenager... that is until an ancient demon attacks her family, kidnaps her cousin, and turns the local police against her...

With nowhere safe to go she has no choice but to team up with an unlikely stranger who seems to be the only person she can trust... but the things he tells her don't seem to make any sense...

As she races around the UK, from the rural villages of Surrey to the great Cathedral Cities of Guildford, Winchester, and London, will she find that ancient legendary weapon, the only one capable of destroying the demon's Army of Shadows?

And, more importantly, will she find it in time to save her friends and family?

For fans of Harry Potter, Hunger Games, and Percy Jackson this real world fantasy novel will keep you on the edge of your seat from the first page to the last word!

Scan this code to get your copy today: